CONTENTS

KT-447-633

Withdrawn From Stock
Dublin City Public Libraries

A Vast Continent

Welcome to Africa, a vast continent covering more than one-fifth of the earth's land surface. Africa's landscape is very varied, ranging from great deserts in the north and south, to equatorial rain forest in its centre, and some savannah and mountain areas.

▼ **This Maasai family are wearing traditional dress.**

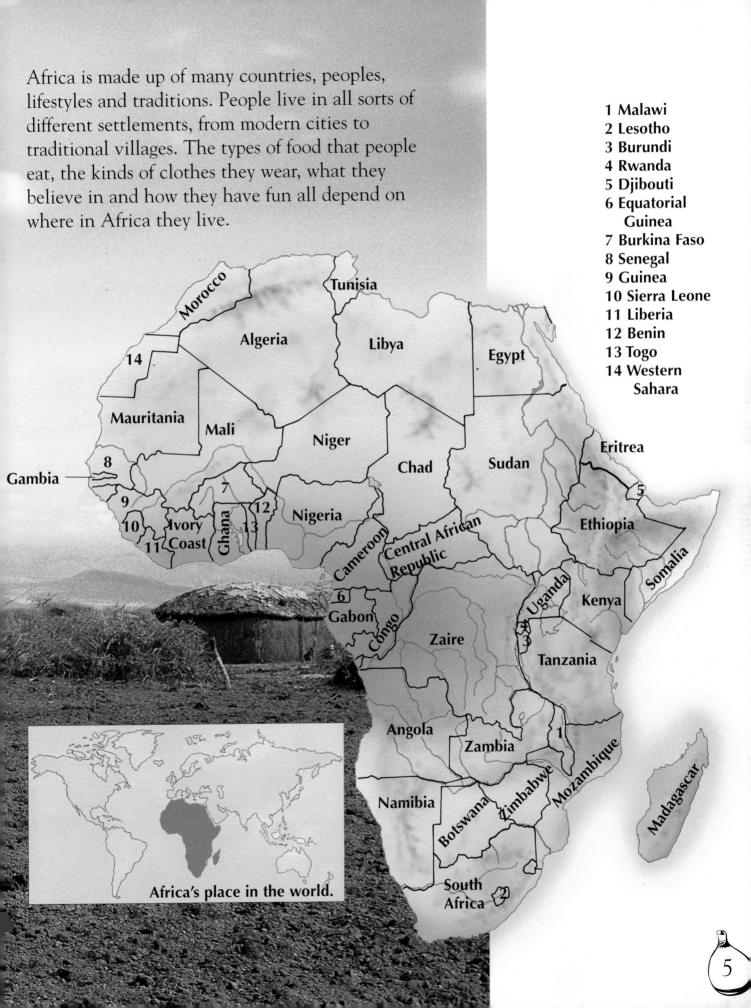

Africa is made up of many countries, peoples, lifestyles and traditions. People live in all sorts of different settlements, from modern cities to traditional villages. The types of food that people eat, the kinds of clothes they wear, what they believe in and how they have fun all depend on where in Africa they live.

1 Malawi
2 Lesotho
3 Burundi
4 Rwanda
5 Djibouti
6 Equatorial
  Guinea
7 Burkina Faso
8 Senegal
9 Guinea
10 Sierra Leone
11 Liberia
12 Benin
13 Togo
14 Western
   Sahara

Morocco
Tunisia
Algeria
Libya
Egypt
14
Mauritania
Mali
Niger
Chad
Sudan
Eritrea
Gambia
8
9
10
Ivory
Coast
11
Ghana
7
12
13
Nigeria
Cameroon
Central African
Republic
Ethiopia
Somalia
5
6
Gabon
Congo
Uganda
Kenya
Zaire
3
Tanzania
Angola
Zambia
1
Mozambique
Madagascar
Namibia
Zimbabwe
Botswana
South
Africa
2

Africa's place in the world.

Influences from Abroad

Trade has played an important part in shaping Africa's history and culture. The first traders to reach Africa were from Arabia. They traded with people all down the east coast, founding forts and bringing the Muslim religion.

Europeans first traded on the west coast of Africa during the sixteenth century. They came for valuable minerals and for slaves. These slaves were taken across the Atlantic Ocean to be sold in the Americas. They were forced to work in horrific conditions. These slaves took African religions, cooking styles, music and other traditions with them.

▼ **A camel driver in Tunisia. Camels were used to transport goods across the desert.**

In the nineteenth century, Europeans became even more powerful in Africa. In 1884, the European powers agreed to divide up the whole of Africa between them. This explains why the official language of many African countries is a European language.

◄ Two women from Zambia carry salt from the modern mines in traditional baskets.

AFRICAN FOOD

Food traditions throughout Africa are often based on foods that are found locally. In West Africa, fish is a staple diet for communities who live near the coast.

Other peoples living further inland herd sheep, goats and cows which provide them with food. The animals are well cared for and killed for their meat only on very special occasions, such as festivals. The Galla people from southern Ethiopia herd Longhorn Zebu cattle, sheep and horses, as well as growing grain.

▼ **A group of fishermen from Mozambique make sure their nets are not broken. They want to get a good catch.**

Maasai Milk Shake

▲ A Maasai woman from Kenya collects some blood from a cow's neck in a gourd container.

The Maasai are nomadic people. They travel through the savannah of Kenya and Tanzania to find new pastures on which to graze their cattle. An important part of the Maasai diet is milk mixed with blood, which they take from the necks of their animals without causing them harm. This mixture is a nutritious weekly food. The Maasai believe it is greedy to kill cattle for food. Taking some blood from a cow means that it can continue to provide nourishment for the rest of its life. But if a cow is killed, it will provide only a few meals.

Farming the Land

In about 60 per cent of countryside areas, African peoples are subsistence farmers. This means that they grow just enough food to feed their families. Maize, cassava, yam, plantain, beans, rice, kola nuts and palm oil are among the most widely farmed foods. Other farmers grow 'cash crops', such as cocoa, coffee, tea and sugar, which can be sold abroad. Some farmers live in harsh, dry areas where it is difficult to grow crops and drought can sometimes be devastating.

▼ Palm nuts are an important crop in Ghana. They provide palm oil, which can be used for cooking.

Yams are a favourite dish of many West African peoples, such as the Igbo of Nigeria and the Ashanti of Ghana. The yams are pounded with pestles in huge mortars to make a fluffy-textured dish. The yams are then flavoured with a spicy sauce.

Serving Food

Throughout Africa, food is served in many different sorts of containers, from gourd bowls and bottles to metal trays, clay pots and baskets woven from grasses. The Baganda people from Uganda serve their food on banana leaves.

This hollowed-out gourd ▶ is called a *calabash*. It is used to store food, such as beans.

Hot and Spicy

Salt is valuable to people who live in the hot, dry desert regions of Africa. A lot of body salts are lost through sweating, and these need to be replaced as often as possible.

In ancient times, Arab camel caravans travelled through the Sahara, trading gold for salt. At the end of their long journeys, camels licked great pillars of salt, which were provided for them by the roadsides of trading towns.

▼ **These brightly coloured beans, lentils and spices on display at Asmeara market in Eritrea will soon attract customers.**

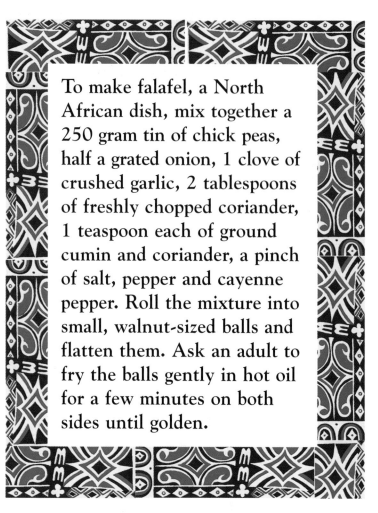

To make falafel, a North African dish, mix together a 250 gram tin of chick peas, half a grated onion, 1 clove of crushed garlic, 2 tablespoons of freshly chopped coriander, 1 teaspoon each of ground cumin and coriander, a pinch of salt, pepper and cayenne pepper. Roll the mixture into small, walnut-sized balls and flatten them. Ask an adult to fry the balls gently in hot oil for a few minutes on both sides until golden.

Spices have long been used to flavour food in Africa. As people have migrated from Africa to other parts of the world, they have introduced hot and spicy African flavours to other places. Spicy cooking is very popular in parts of the USA, where meats are barbecued in an African-style sauce.

▲ A family in Zanzibar, Tanzania, sits down to eat lunch.

CLOTHES AND COSTUME

Many people in Africa today wear Western-style clothes. But there are some people in rural Africa who wear traditional clothes on special occasions. Often people wear a mixture of traditional and Western clothing.

Local Materials

Traditional African clothes are made from local materials. Most cloth is woven from cotton or animal hair, but there are many more unusual types of material. Some peoples wear clothes made from animal skins or plant fibres such as raffia. In Uganda, Rwanda and parts of the Congo Basin, some people use bark to make a type of cloth.

Yoruba women in small Nigerian villages make brightly coloured cotton cloths with cassava-paste designs. Each pattern has a special meaning. The women get ideas for designs from the things around them, such as combs, birds or plants, and from sayings. The cloths are then coloured with natural dyes from the indigo plant.

▼ **This woman in The Gambia carries piles of tie-dyed cloth on her head to keep her hands free.**

14

Berber women in parts of North Africa weave sheep wool into cloth. The men sew the cloth into long, hooded tunics which keep out the icy cold in the high Atlas mountains. The men also knit and crochet woollen trousers for themselves.

▲ A bustling market in Burundi. Some people are wearing Western-style clothes. Others are wearing a brightly coloured local cloth.

In parts of Ghana, men are responsible for weaving complicated designs from silk threads on narrow looms. The long *kente* strips are then sewn together into large cloths, which the chiefs wear at special ceremonies.

Special Occasions

▼ **A weaver makes narrow *kente* strips on a hand loom in Ghana. One day he will teach these skills to his sons.**

Zulu people from South Africa wear animal skins on special occasions. First, the skins are tanned and dried. Then, they are made into skirts and beads are sewn on to them. Women wear the skirts for ceremonial dances. Some of the beadwork jangles musically as they dance each step.

Ceremonial clothes are important in many African cultures. Often, different colours, shapes and decorations all have special meanings. In Benin City in Nigeria, the chiefs wear red at court because it is associated with power and protects against evil.

▶ **Esther Mahlango, an artist from South Africa, paints the *adobe* wall of a house. The pattern is based on the beadwork designs found on traditional clothing.**

Masks

In many African cultures, masks are worn during dances and important occasions. Mask-makers carefully craft the masks, often from wood or animal skin. The masks are usually worn by men.

One group of women who wear masks is the Mende women's society in Sierra Leone. Senior officials wear wooden masks to celebrate girls becoming women. The features on the masks are signs of beauty, such as a high forehead, thin eyes, complicated hairstyles, a small pointed chin and, most importantly, rolls of fat around the neck.

▼ **This *Shangan* dancer from Zimbabwe is wearing a brown and white painted mask, complete with beard.**

▶ **The dust flies as this ceremonial masked dancer from Malawi shows off his skill.**

Beads and Bangles

Most African peoples traditionally wear some form of jewellery as part of their costume. Many different materials are worn as jewellery, such as coral, glass beads, shells and metals. San women of the Kalahari Desert make tiny beads from broken ostrich eggshells. These beads are used to decorate the edges of clothes, or headbands. Today, more modern materials are also used, such as buttons or bottle tops.

In many cultures jewellery is worn to show the wealth of the person wearing it. In North Africa, Berber women wear valuable coins sewn on to their head-dresses. Wealthy Fulani women from Nigeria wear much of their family's riches on their bodies.

◀ **This young Maasai girl is wearing a traditional collar and headband made from hundreds of tiny, brightly coloured beads.**

In South Africa, jewellery has traditionally been used to pass on messages. Zulu girls weave necklaces of white beads with pendants of different coloured beads hanging down. Each colour has a special meaning and can be 'read'. The girls send these necklaces to the boys they love. Boys can wear several of these 'love letters' from different girls at the same time.

▼ These Muslim women in Eritrea, are wearing *arusa* wedding masks decorated with silver jewellery to cover their faces.

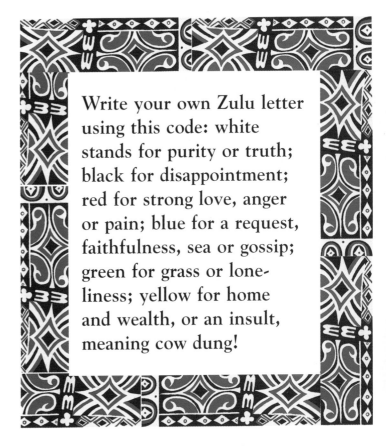

Write your own Zulu letter using this code: white stands for purity or truth; black for disappointment; red for strong love, anger or pain; blue for a request, faithfulness, sea or gossip; green for grass or loneliness; yellow for home and wealth, or an insult, meaning cow dung!

MUSIC AND DANCE

All over Africa, music and dance play an essential part in marking important events such as birth, marriage and death. A huge range of instruments are played, from drums and rattles to flutes and xylophones. Traditional instruments are carefully crafted from local materials such as wood, gourds, beans and seeds, moth cocoons, recycled bottle tops and metal fencing, and animal skins and horns.

▼ **A musician in Namibia plays a simple mouth harp.**

Drumming a Message

Drums have always been an important feature of African music. Yoruba people from Nigeria send messages across vast distances, up to 30 kilometres, using 'talking drums'. These tall, goblet-shaped drums have two membranes which are joined together by strings. The player skilfully squeezes the strings while beating one end of the drum. This makes high and low sounds, which sound like the Yoruba language.

▶ *Ninga* **drummers from Burundi beat out a rhythm while a dancer spins athletically in mid-air.**

In Cameroon, some musicians play portable xylophones. The sound-boxes are made out of gourds and the keys are made from wood. In the past, the chief used to take four musicians with him on long journeys. The musicians walked ahead and played the xylophones to show how important the chief was.

In many parts of Africa, music is used to mark important religious occasions. In Morocco, the *Nfir*, a trumpet that is 1.5 metres long signals the end of Ramadan, the Muslim month of fasting, with long blasts of sound.

◀ **This musician from Chad really fills his cheeks with air to blow this wind instrument.**

You don't have to go to Africa to listen to African music. Your local music store may have a selection of African music. Musicians from Africa such as Youssou N'Dour have teamed up with well-known Western musicians, such as Neneh Cherry, to produce a rich mix of both cultures.

▲ **Youssou N'Dour from Senegal mixes African and Western styles of music at a pop concert.**

Around the World

Many African instruments have travelled all over the world as people have moved from place to place. Banjos are believed to have developed from stringed instruments called *coras*. When slaves were transported from Africa, they took traditional styles of music with them. These slaves created new musical styles which became a base for popular music all around the world. Jazz, blues and rock and pop music all grew out of this type of music.

The Importance of Dance

Music is often accompanied by dance. Many African dances take place at certain times of the year to mark special occasions.

In some parts of Africa it is important for dancers to move particular parts of the body. The way that people walk, stand or dance is believed to show the strength of their character.

▼ *Gitega* **drummers in Burundi play at a dance competition to attract good spirits.**

In south-west Angola, the Humbi and Handa peoples sometimes perform a *Nkili* dance, where the men leap high in the air and are caught by women. The women have to be very strong and the dancers have to be careful, using very precise dance movements.

Dance competitions are also popular in parts of Africa. The Wodaabe people of Niger hold competitions judged by women to choose the most beautiful man. The men take a long time to prepare for the competition, painting their faces to make their eyes and their teeth stand out. The women circle round the group of dancers, clapping their hands.

Masked Dancing

Dancers often wear masks. In solo masked dancing, each movement is designed to pass on a special message to the audience. A masked dancer is like an actor, using special movements, dance steps and styles of walking to create a particular character.

The Dogon peoples of Mali have a masked society, called *Awa*, who perform complicated dances accompanied by chants in a secret language. At funerals boy dancers wear wooden masks made up of high double crosses. The masks almost touch the ground as the dancers move up and down, backwards and forwards. The dancers beat the ground around the dead body, to ask for its forgiveness.

▼ **Dogon dancers in Mali wear traditional masks to mourn the dead at a funeral ceremony, called a *dama*.**

Team Dancing

Team dances are popular throughout Africa. The teams are organized by a leader who is chosen for his or her dance skill and creativity. Leaders train their teams to perform together after them in time to the music.

Most importantly, dance is a way of getting people in a community together. Dances are used to mark important occasions, but they can also be a lot of fun.

▼ **These people in South Africa have joined together in the streets to dance and celebrate a special occasion.**

RELIGION AND FESTIVALS

Africa has many folk beliefs and traditions. Followers of traditional religions believe in a creator god who is responsible for making the world. This creator is usually male, but some groups do believe in female gods.

Many African peoples believe that they can communicate with the creator through the spirits of their ancestors. By making offerings to these ancestral spirits people can ask the creator to help them produce a good harvest or bring up healthy children. Ancestors are honoured at *Egungun*, an annual Yoruba festival which takes place in June. This festival marks the time for harvesting new crops of yam. Spectators ask masked dancers representing their ancestors for blessings.

▼ **Music often plays an important part in religious ceremonies and festivals. These drummers perform traditional music at the annual *Wli Asuatsu* Festival in Ghana.**

Tyi Wara Masquerades

All religious teachings tell us how to behave. The Bamana people from Mali tell an important myth about Tyi Wara, a half-man, half-antelope. According to the myth, Tyi Wara taught the first peoples how to grow crops. When he saw wasted grain he hid himself, and his disappointment, in the earth until they carved dance head-dresses in his memory. Tyi Wara masquerades encourage people to work hard and succeed in farming.

▲ This fishing festival in Nigeria is held to ask the spirits for plenty of fish in the year to come.

Food, clothing and music are all closely linked to traditional African religions. There are no holy books to help teach these religions. Instead, patterns and colours on masks and clothing worn during masquerades and festivals all have religious meanings. The Ashanti people in Ghana wrap their dead in *adinkra* cloths to ease the way to the afterlife. The cloths are printed with repeating patterns from pieces of carved gourd, which bring good luck. The patterns can be read like poems.

▼ **Tissent women hold out their hands as a sign of respect while singing in the folklore festival at Marrakesh, in Morocco.**

On which day of the week were you born? Use the key below to find out what your name would be in Ghana.

Birthday	Girls	Boys
Monday	Adwoa	Kojo
Tuesday	Abena	Kwabena
Wednesday	Ekua	Kweku
Thursday	Yaa	Yaw
Friday	Efia	Kofi
Saturday	Ama	Kwame
Sunday	Akosua	Kwesi

What's in a Name?

Naming new-born children is important to all cultures of the world. In Nigeria, the Yoruba people name their children at a special naming ceremony when the child is eight days old. In Ghana, children are named immediately after birth, according to which day of the week they are born and whether they are a girl or a boy.

◀ **A young girl dances to celebrate growing up at a special ceremony in Ghana.**

33

Christianity

There have been Christians in the northern parts of Africa since the Christian religion first began. The image of the cross is an important symbol for Christians all over the world. In Lalibela, Ethiopia, during the thirteenth century, the spectacular cross-shaped church of St George was built out of solid rock. The colonial powers of Europe spread Christianity to more peoples in Africa. Today, many African people are Christians.

▼ These priests from Ethiopia are wearing ceremonial robes. They have covered their heads with white turbans.

► **Children in Kenya celebrate the end of the day's fasting during the holy month of Ramadan.**

The Spread of Islam

Islam travelled to Africa from Arab countries during the seventh century, when Arabs conquered and converted the peoples in the north. Today, many people in North and East Africa are Muslims. They keep the 'five pillars of Islam': fasting between sunrise and sunset during Ramadan; praying five times a day; giving alms; going on pilgrimages if possible; and believing in Allah, the one god.

GAMES AND TOYS

Many African games are based around myths and legends. Chasing games and board games are very popular in Africa.

Mancala is a board game from West Africa. It is played in a similar way to draughts but on boards with cup-like dents carved into them. Two people usually play on a two-row, eight-cup *mancala* board. Each player owns half the board and fifty-two pebbles.

▼ **These Ugandan children have made dents in the soil and are using nuts to play a game called** *bao.*

The aim of *mancala* is to capture the opponent's pieces by picking up one cupful of pebbles and spreading them clockwise in each cup, taking all pebbles from the last cup. *Mancala* is a competitive game of skill, played at top speed, usually with a noisy audience of supporters.

Many African games have travelled to other parts of the world. The walls of ancient Egyptian tombs have paintings of people playing a board game called *senet*, which was rather like draughts. Hopscotch, noughts and crosses and backgammon all began as African games. The rules may have changed a little, but the ideas are still the same.

▲ These young men in Senegal are playing a game of draughts. The pieces are made out of wood.

Homemade Toys

African peoples rarely waste materials, and often recycle them. Nigerian men make toy cars by cutting and bending sheets of empty oil cans into the right shapes. Wheels made from the round tops of aerosol cans are then added to the frames.

In South Africa, men create complicated moving wire toys for their children from lengths of recycled fencing. These toys are made in many shapes, ranging from cars with moving wheels, bonnets and aerials to crocodiles with snapping jaws and moving legs. South African country-women often make dolls for their children from the used husks of maize, with clothing made from material and decorated with beadwork.

Dosu is a game played in Nigeria. The players each make a sand castle and choose someone to hide a small object in one of the castles while they turn their backs. Then each player chooses a pile. The winner is the person who finds the object.

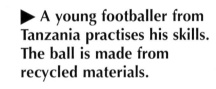

► **A young footballer from Tanzania practises his skills. The ball is made from recycled materials.**

► **This boy in Guinea is riding a home-made scooter.**

Sport

We know from paintings on the walls of ancient Egyptian tombs that wrestling, running and horse-riding have long been popular African sports. Today, people still like to watch and take part in them.

Wrestling is a popular sport amongst Nuba boys and men in North Africa, where the fights can be very fierce. The aim of the match is for one wrestler to pin his opponent's shoulders to the ground. These wrestling matches often attract huge crowds and many fighters are treated like celebrities.

▼ Two Dinka men demonstrate their skill in a wrestling match in Sudan.

▲ **Athletes battle for first place in a track competion in Nairobi, Kenya.**

Many African athletes have won medals in competitions world-wide. Abebe Bikila won the Olympic marathon, running barefoot, in 1960 and in 1964. In 1982, John Mwebi of Kenya, and Ohene Karikari and George Danial of Ghana all won medals. More recently, Wilson Kipketer, originally from Kenya, won a gold medal for the 200 metre race, running for Norway in the 1997 Commonwealth games in Athens.

STORY TIME

There has always been a great tradition of storytelling in Africa. Creation myths describe how and why the world was made. Dilemma tales have no ending, so listeners must choose the correct course of action to take. Trickster tales are designed to make the listener think before they act. Stories are told with great skill, to entertain and make people think. In some villages, people still gather together in the twilight to hear stories.

Many stories travelled with Africans who were captured and sold to the slave trade. Telling these stories must have given the slaves courage to survive the terrible conditions. The tales described characters such as Anansi the spider and Hare and Tortoise, who have become popular all over the world.

THE BOX
A Story from South Africa

Long, long ago, a farmer owned a magnificent herd of seven black and white cows. The cattle always gave the farmer such rich, creamy milk that he soon became the envy of his neighbours. One morning, the farmer went to milk his animals, just as he did every day. But he was amazed to find that the cows had no milk to give him.

'Hmm,' he said. 'This is strange. Someone must have stolen my milk during the night. Tonight I will hide myself in some bushes and sit up, all night, to watch for the thief.'

The farmer made himself comfortable and sat patiently watching, and waiting. Soon he drifted off into a dreamy sleep. In his dream, the farmer saw seven beautiful girls, climbing down from the sky on seven starry ropes, each carrying a gourd bowl. When the girls reached the ground they went up to the cows and started to milk them.

A fly fluttered past the farmer's nose and woke him up. As he wiped the sleep from his eyes, the farmer thought 'What a strange dream,' and turned to look at his cattle. Imagine the farmer's surprise when he saw each one of his cows being milked by a beautiful girl!

The farmer ran towards the nearest girl and grabbed her by the waist, making her drop her gourd. The other girls climbed up the starry ropes as fast as they could, and vanished.

43

The Box

The girl struggled, but could not escape. The farmer was strong and he had fallen in love with her. He asked the girl to marry him there and then, still holding her tightly.

The girl thought carefully for a moment and then answered him. 'I will marry you, but…' (there is always a 'but' in such tales). 'But' she said, 'you must not, under any circumstances, look in this box, not until I say that you may.'

'Look in the box!' thought the farmer. He hadn't even noticed the box that she clutched to her before, so he could easily promise not to look inside. The farmer readily agreed.

The couple lived and worked happily together for a long time. But (sometimes there are even two buts in such tales!) the thought of what might be in the box nagged away at the farmer.

The box sat in the corner of the farmer's hut and began to play on his mind. It was such an ordinary, plain wooden thing with no interesting features. Why couldn't he look inside it? People who are truly in love should have no secrets from each other. He had no secrets from his wife. It wasn't fair of her to keep this private thing between them. The farmer would never really be contented, with this box, there, unopened.

What if he opened it just a crack? Oh, to open the box! This thought took hold of the farmer until he could control it no longer. He decided that he must open it. The farmer ran into his hut, picked up the box, and pulled open the lid.

The Box

To the farmer's amazement, the box was quite empty. What a fuss his wife had made, about an empty box! The farmer laughed because now he would not have to think about the box and what was inside it. Now he could be truly happy. The farmer replaced the box in the corner of the hut, where it had been since he had married his wife. Just at that moment, his beautiful wife came in. She looked at the box and then she looked sadly at her husband.

'Oh,' she sighed. 'What have you done? You have opened the box! I told you that was the one thing you must not do until I said you may. Now I have to leave you.'

The farmer did not understand. 'What? Leave me? You can see there's nothing in the box, it's empty.'

'Ah,' said the farmer's wife. 'That box contains all the riches, the beauties and wonders of the world. You came so close to seeing them, but you could not wait. Now you will always be blind to them.' She picked up the box, left the hut and was never seen again.

The poor farmer only knew how to see things immediately before his eyes, such as his cattle and their good milk. There are many more precious things in the world, such as friendship, hope, and trust. It takes more time and it is much harder to appreciate these things. Unfortunately some people will always be blind to them, but you and I know how important they are.

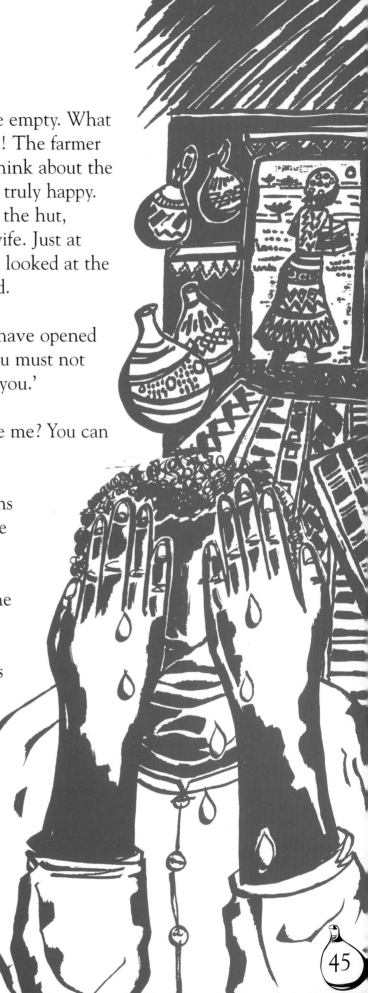

TOPIC WEB

HISTORY

- Researching slavery
- Migrations of people
- Researching colonialism
- Benin
- Ancient Egypt

R.E.

- Festivals and masquerades
- Role of music
- Role of clothing
- Islam
- Christianity

SCIENCE

- Sound
- Nutritional value of food

GEOGRAPHY

- Clothes and their purpose
- Types of weather and their advantages and disadvantages
- Types of food grown in different countries
- Farming

DESIGN AND TECHNOLOGY

- Design a mask
- Design a necklace
- Clothes for different temperatures

TRADITIONS FROM AFRICA

P.E./DANCE/DRAMA

- Team dancing
- Dance competitions
- Masquerade

ENGLISH

- Library skills
- Creative writing
- Myths
- Poems
- Signs and symbols
- Importance of naming

MUSIC

- Exploring rhythm
- Making sounds
- Percussion instruments

MATHS

- Deciphering codes
- Repeating patterns

ART AND CRAFT

- Mixing colours
- Tie Dye
- Wool and weaving
- People and clothes
- Textures of materials

GLOSSARY

Adobe Sun-dried brick, made from clay.

Ancestors Family members who have died.

Cash crops Produced for sale, not for food.

Cassava-paste The boiled root of the cassava plant, used to decorate dyed cotton fabrics.

Drought Long periods without rain.

Equatorial rain forest Areas of forest that have heavy rainfall.

Gourd The dried and emptied rind of a trailing or climbing fruit plant, used to make bowls, bottles and musical instruments.

Masquerades Celebrations where people dress up in costumes and masks.

Migrations Movements of people from one place to another.

Nomadic Travelling from place to place in search of pasture for grazing animals.

Pestles Club-shaped instruments used for pounding food in a bowl or mortar.

Pilgrimages Journeys to holy places.

Portable Easy to carry.

Raffia Fibre from the leaves of palm trees that is used to make mats, baskets and hats.

Savannah Grassland areas with few or no trees.

Settlers People who go to live in a new country.

Slaves People who are owned by another person.

Staple diet The important or main parts of people's everyday food.

Tanning A way of preparing leather .

Tunics Short-sleeved close-fitting clothes that reach to about the knees.

FURTHER INFORMATION

Non-fiction:
Africa by Peadar Cremin and Colm Regan (Wayland, 1996)

Eyewitness Guide: Africa by Yvonne Ayo (Dorling Kindersley, 1995)

Kenya (Country Insights series) by Dunne, Kairi & Nyanjom (Wayland, 1997)

Traditions Around the World series (Wayland, 1995)

Fiction and Poetry:
African Stories Retold by Robert Hull (Wayland, 1992)

Can I buy a Slice of Sky? Poems from Black, Asian and American Indian cultures edited by Grace Nichols (Hodder, 1996)

Photopack:
Feeling Good About Far-Away Friends: Daily Life of a Maasai Family in Kenya (Leeds Development Education Centre, 1995)

INDEX Page numbers in **bold** refer to photographs.